now you're cookin'
VEGETARIAN DISHES

© 2007 Rebo International b.v., Lisse, The Netherlands

This title is a revision of title Vegetarian dishes that was published by Rebo Productions in 1998.

Recipes and photographs on pages 10–11, 12–13, 22–23, 18–19, 20–21, 26–27, 32–33, 36–37, 40–41, 42–43, 44–45, 56–57, 60–61, 62–63, 70–71, 72–73, 74–75, 76–77, 78–79, 80–81, 84–85, 94–95: © Ceres Verlag, Rudolf-August Oetker KG, Bielefeld, Germany

All other recipes and photographs: © Quadrillion Publishing Ltd, Godalming, Surrey

Design and layout: Minkowsky Graphics, Enkhuizen, The Netherlands

Typesetting: AdAm Studio, Prague, The Czech Republic

Cover design: Minkowsky Graphics, Enkhuizen, The Netherlands

Translation: Stephen Challacombe

Proofreading: Sarah Dunham

ISBN: 978-90-366-2242-4

now you're cookin'

VEGETARIAN DISHES

THIS BOOK JUST MAKES YOU WANNA COOK –

REBO
PUBLISHERS

Introduction

An ever-growing number of people are turning to vegetarianism for a variety of reasons – some out of concern for the well-being of animals, others for environmental reasons and many for health reasons.

Studies suggest that vegetarians are significantly less likely to develop cancer at an early age than meat eaters. Added to that, because vegetarians and vegans are often slimmer than meat eaters, eat more fiber and more complex carbohydrates in the form of wholegrain cereals, nuts and pulses and also eat fewer saturated fats (predominantly found in animal products), they enjoy lower levels of blood cholesterol and therefore heart disease, and have a higher level of protection against several bowel diseases.

But besides offering a healthy diet, if well-balanced, vegetarian food provides the opportunity to enjoy a whole new taste experience beyond the confines of the traditional meal. This is the chance to exploit to the full the wealth of fresh and exotic fruits, vegetables and herbs now freely available all year round, as well as the heady mix of spices and flavorings drawn from the cuisines of the world. Then there are those all-important, nourishing staple foods which offer enormous potential for creating imaginative and delicious dishes – nutty grains such as couscous and wild rice, toothsome tomato and spinach-flavored pasta, sweet nuts such as pistachios and pecans and tender legumes including flageolet beans and chick-peas.

This book presents a collection of exciting recipes for all those who enjoy good food, whether they are committed vegetarians or not. Sample the vegetarian highlights of international cooking, such as Spanish Gazpacho soup, Greek Tzatziki dip, Indian Vegetable Curry and Middle Eastern Tabouleh salad, or savor the delights of some contemporary creations including Watercress and Mushroom Paté, Parsnip Fritters, Potato and Zucchini Gratin, Chocolate and Almond Biscuits and Cashew Ice Cream. So, why not go vegetarian today!

Conversion tables

Measurements

teaspoons	tablespoons	cups	fluid ounces	milliliters
1				5
3	1	1/16	1/2	15
6	2	1/8	1	30
	4	1/4	2	60
	5 1/3	1/3	2 1/2	75
	6	3/8	3	90
	8	1/2	4	125
		2/3	5	150
		3/4	6	175
		1	8	237
		1 1/2	12	355
		2	16	473
		3	24	710
		4	32	946

Oven Temperatures

150 °C	300 °F
160 °C	325 °F
180 °C	350 °F
190 °C	375 °F
200 °C	400 °F
220 °C	425 °F
230 °C	450 °F

Method

Melt the margarine in a large pan and add the fennel, carrots, onion, garlic, parsnip and salt and pepper. Cover and allow to sweat over a very low heat for 10–15 minutes, stirring occasionally. Add the parsley, tomato purée, potato and stock. Stir well, bring to the boil, then simmer for 20–30 minutes, until the vegetables are cooked and tender, stirring occasionally. Just before serving, add the peas. Bring back to the boil and serve immediately. Ladle into warmed soup tureens to serve.

Garden Vegetable Soup

Ingredients

1 tbsp margarine

½ head of fennel, finely chopped

3 medium carrots, diced

1 onion, chopped

2–3 cloves garlic, crushed

1 parsnip, diced

Salt and freshly ground black pepper

2 tsp dried parsley

1 tbsp tomato purée

1 large potato, diced

2 quarts vegetable stock

2 oz frozen peas

Serving suggestion

Serve with crusty rolls or slices of French bread.

Variations

If fennel is not available, use 2 or 3 sticks of finely chopped celery. Use sweetcorn kernels in place of peas. Use 1 large sweet potato in place of standard potato.

Method

Cook the split peas in the stock in a saucepan for 10–15 minutes, stirring occasionally. Meanwhile, melt the margarine in a separate pan, add the onion, celery and leeks and cook for a few minutes, stirring occasionally.

Add to the peas and stock together with the potatoes and carrot and bring back to the boil. Reduce the heat, cover and simmer for 30 minutes, stirring occasionally. Remove from the heat and cool slightly, then purée in a food processor or blender until smooth. Return the blended mixture to the rinsed-out pan and reheat gently until piping hot, stirring occasionally. Season to taste with salt and pepper and ladle into warmed soup bowls to serve. Garnish with leek slices.

Ingredients

8 oz split peas

2 quarts vegetable stock or water and a stock

cube

4 tbsp vegetable margarine

1 large onion, chopped

3 sticks celery, chopped

2 leeks, thinly sliced

2 medium potatoes, diced

1 medium carrot, finely chopped

Salt and freshly ground black pepper

Leek slices, to garnish

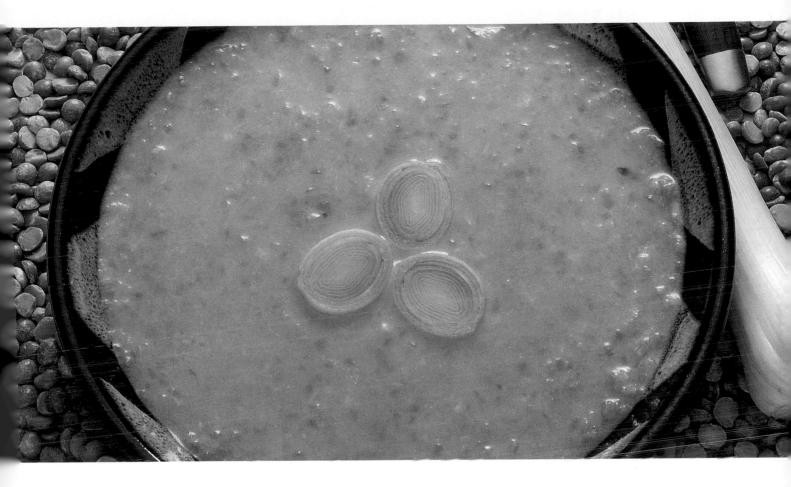

Split Pea Soup

Serving suggestion

Serve with fresh bread or bread rolls.

Variations

Use green or brown lentils in place of split peas. Use sweet potatoes in place

of standard potatoes. Use 1 parsnip in place of the carrot.

Method

Place the rye and pearl barley in a bowl and cover with cold water. Leave to soak overnight. Place the prepared vegetables in a large saucepan with the soaked grains, soaking liquid and 1 3/4 cups water. Add the salt, fennel seeds, tarragon and pepper and stir to mix. Bring to a boil, then cover, reduce the heat and simmer for about 20–30 minutes, or until the vegetables and grains are cooked and tender, stirring occasionally. Stir in the milk, cream and dill, reheat gently, then ladle into warmed soup bowls to serve.

Ingredients

3 ½ oz rye grains

3 ½ oz pearl barley

7 oz sauerkraut, thinly sliced

2 green peppers, seeded and sliced

1 leek, thinly sliced

2 sticks celery, thinly sliced

4 firm tomatoes, sliced

4 young carrots, thinly sliced

2 tsp salt

1 tsp fennel seeds

1 tsp chopped fresh tarragon

Freshly ground black pepper, to taste

½ cup milk

½ cup sour cream

1 tbsp chopped fresh dill

Mixed Vegetable and Barley Soup

Method

Heat the oil in a large saucepan, add the onions and cook gently for 10–15 minutes, until softened, stirring occasionally. Meanwhile, cut away the corn from the cobs with a sharp knife, working lengthways down each cob. Add the sweetcorn kernels to the onions with the stock and stir to mix. Bring to the boil, then reduce the heat. Cover and simmer for 10 minutes, until the sweetcorn is cooked and tender, stirring occasionally. Remove the pan from the heat and cool slightly, then purée in a food processor or blender until smooth. Return the soup to the rinsed-out pan, add the cream, pepper and nutmeg and reheat gently until hot, stirring occasionally. Ladle into warmed soup bowls and serve garnished with parsley.

Ingredients

2 tbsp olive oil

6 onions, sliced

6 corn on the cob

4 cups vegetable stock

6 tbsp double cream

Freshly ground black pepper, to taste

Freshly grated nutmeg, to taste

Chopped fresh parsley, to garnish

Cream of Sweetcorn Soup

Method

Plunge the tomatoes into a bowl of boiling water, leave for 1 minute, then plunge into a bowl of cold water. Remove and discard the skins and seeds. Set aside.

Chop the onion and pepper and place in a food processor or blender with the tomatoes, garlic, cucumber, wine vinegar, oil and tomato juice.

Purée until smooth and well mixed. Add the lime juice and seasoning to taste and blend to mix. Pour the soup into a glass dish, cover and chill until required. Ladle into soup bowls to serve and garnish each serving with a few croutons.

Gazpacho

Ingredients

1 lb ripe tomatoes

1 small onion

1 small green pepper, seeded

1 clove garlic, crushed

¼ medium cucumber

1 tbsp red wine vinegar

1 tbsp olive oil

14-oz can tomato juice

1–2 tbsp lime juice

Salt and freshly ground black pepper

Croutons, to garnish

Serving suggestion

Serve with lightly buttered wholemeal bread.

Variations

Use plum tomatoes or yellow tomatoes in place of standard tomatoes. Use 1 small leek in place of the onion. Use cider vinegar in place of red wine vinegar.

Cook's tip

If the soup is too thick, add more tomato juice.

Method

Melt the butter in a saucepan over a low heat, add the onion and cook until soft but not coloured, stirring occasionally. Increase the heat, add the mushrooms and cook quickly for 2 minutes, stirring frequently. Add the chopped watercress and stir for about 30 seconds, until it becomes limp. Place the contents of the pan in a food processor or blender together with the cheese and shoyu. Blend until smooth and well mixed. Stir in the caraway seeds and pepper to taste. Place in individual ramekin dishes or one large serving dish, cover and chill for at least 2 hours, until firm, before serving. Garnish with lime wedges.

Ingredients

2 tbsp butter

1 onion, finely chopped

3 oz field mushrooms, finely chopped

1 bunch of watercress, finely chopped

4 oz low-fat curd cheese

A few drops of shoyu (Japanese soy sauce)

½ tsp caraway seeds

Freshly ground black pepper

Lime wedges, to garnish

Watercress and Mushroom Paté

Serving suggestion

Serve with thin slices of lightly buttered brown bread or toast.

Variations

Use fresh wild mushrooms in place of field mushrooms. Use arugula in

place of watercress. Use 4 shallots in place of the onion.

Cook's tip

It may be necessary to stir the contents of the food processor or blender

several times, since the mixture should be fairly thick.

soups & starters

17

Method

Brush the peppers all over with oil, then place on a baking tray.

Bake in a preheated oven at 425°F for about 15 minutes, turning every 5 minutes, until blistered and brown. Remove the peppers from the oven, cover with a damp cloth and allow to cool slightly. Remove and discard the skin, seeds and cores from the peppers. Cut the flesh into strips, then season with salt and pepper. Cut each of the cheeses into equal sized pieces. Place the sheep's cheese on the yellow pepper strips, the Gorgonzola on the green pepper and the Gouda or Cheddar on the red pepper. Thread onto cocktail sticks or skewers and serve.

Cheese and Pepper Bites

Ingredients

1 yellow pepper

1 red pepper

1 green pepper

1 tsp olive oil

Salt and freshly ground black pepper

3 oz sheep's cheese

3 oz Gorgonzola

3 oz Gouda or Cheddar cheese

Serving suggestions

Serve with a mixed leaf or chopped salad or crusty bread.

Variations

Use 1 beefsteak tomato in place of the red pepper. There is no need to roast the tomato – simply remove the seeds and cut into strips. Use Stilton in place of Gorgonzola.

Method

Wash the beans and place in a bowl. Cover with water, add the thyme sprig and leave to soak overnight. Drain. Pour the stock into a pan and add the beans. Press the cloves into the peeled onion, then add the onion, garlic and bay leaf to the stock and beans. Stir to mix. Bring to the boil, then cover, reduce the heat and simmer for 1½ hours, until the beans are cooked and tender, stirring occasionally. Strain through a sieve or colander and reserve the beans. Discard the stock, onion and garlic. Meanwhile, for the dressing, place the onion in a bowl and sprinkle with sea salt. Leave for 10 minutes to allow the salt to be absorbed. Add the crushed garlic to the onion with the mustard, oregano, wine vinegar, oil, parsley and pepper to taste. Mix the dressing with the beans, cover and leave to marinate in the refrigerator for several hours before serving. Serve, garnished with fresh herb sprigs.

Ingredients

7 oz mixed brown and white beans

1 sprig of fresh thyme

1 3/4 cups vegetable stock

2 whole cloves

1 onion

2 cloves garlic

1 bay leaf

Fresh herb sprigs, to garnish

For the dressing

1 onion, sliced

Sea salt, to sprinkle

2 cloves garlic, crushed

½–1 tsp Dijon mustard

½–1 tsp dried oregano

4 tbsp red wine vinegar

5 tbsp olive oil

Marinated Beans

1 bunch of fresh parsley, finely chopped

Freshly ground black pepper, to taste

Serving suggestion

Serve with garlic bread.

Variations

Use wholegrain mustard in place of Dijon mustard. Use walnut or hazelnut oil
in place of olive oil. Use fresh basil in place of parsley.

Method

Cut the cucumber in half lengthways, then remove and discard the seeds and cut the flesh into small cubes. Place in a bowl. Add the yogurt or crème fraîche and garlic and stir to mix well. Add the mint, olive oil and salt and pepper and mix well. Spoon into a dish and serve garnished with fresh parsley sprigs.

Tzatziki

Serving suggestion

Serve with pita bread, black olives and fresh vegetable crudités.

Ingredients

1 lb 2 oz cucumber

1 lb 2 oz plain yogurt or crème fraîche

1 clove garlic, thinly sliced

2 tbsp finely chopped fresh mint

Olive oil, to taste

Salt and freshly ground black pepper, to taste

Fresh parsley sprigs, to garnish

Variations

Use Greek yogurt if you like. Use chopped fresh mixed herbs in place of mint.

Cook's tip

The cucumber can be coarsely grated rather than cut into cubes.

Method

Cook the onion in a little water in a saucepan until softened. Drain.

Peel the cooked potatoes and mash in a bowl with the milk, butter and

salt and pepper to taste. Add the drained onion and mix well. Divide the

mixture in half and make nests on a greased baking sheet. Crack an egg

into each nest and sprinkle with grated cheese. Bake in a preheated oven

at 400°F for 20–25 minutes, or until the eggs are set. Serve, garnished

with parsley.

Ingredients

1 onion, finely chopped

1 lb potatoes, cooked in their skins

A little milk

A knob of butter

Salt and freshly ground black pepper

2 medium eggs

1 oz Cheddar cheese, grated

Chopped fresh parsley, to garnish

Potato Nests

Serving suggestions

Serve with beans and grilled tomatoes or a salad.

Variations

The nests can be filled with chopped leftover nut roast mixed with

a mushroom or tomato sauce and a few freshly chopped herbs. Use

sweet potatoes in place of standard potatoes.

Method

Cut the Chinese cabbage into four and rinse thoroughly. Cook in a saucepan of salted boiling water for about 6 minutes. Drain the cabbage, then place it in a greased ovenproof dish. Lay the mushroom slices over the cabbage and season to taste with salt and pepper. In a bowl, mix the crème fraîche and yogurt together, beat in the eggs and season with salt and pepper. Add grated nutmeg and curry powder, stir well, then pour the sauce over the mushrooms. Sprinkle with the grated cheese and cook in a preheated oven at 400°F for about 30 minutes, until golden brown. Serve hot.

Chinese Cabbage Gratin

Ingredients

1 lb 10 oz Chinese cabbage

9 oz mushrooms, sliced

Salt and freshly ground black pepper

5 ½ oz crème fraîche

5 ½ oz full cream plain yogurt

2 medium eggs

Grated nutmeg, to taste

Curry powder, to taste

3 ½ oz mature Gouda cheese, grated

Serving suggestions

Serve with a mixed leaf salad or baked potatoes.

Variations

Use zucchini in place of mushrooms. Use Cheddar cheese in place of Gouda. Use green cabbage in place of Chinese cabbage.

Method

Mix the almonds, hazelnuts and pecan nuts together with the breadcrumbs and cheese in a bowl. Set aside. In another bowl, mix the beaten egg with the sherry, onion, ginger, parsley, chilli and red pepper. Combine with the nut mixture and add the salt and pepper. Mix well. If the mixture is too dry, add a little more sherry or milk. Form the mixture into small 1-inch balls. Arrange the balls on a well greased baking tray and bake in a non-preheated oven at 350°F for about 20–25 minutes, until golden brown. Serve warm or cold, garnished with lemon or lime slices.

Ingredients

2 ¼ oz ground almonds

2 ¼ oz ground hazelnuts

2 ¼ oz pecan nuts

3 oz fresh wholemeal breadcrumbs

4 oz Cheddar cheese, grated

1 egg, beaten

4–5 tbsp dry sherry or 2 tbsp milk
and 3 tbsp dry sherry

1 small onion, finely chopped

1 tbsp grated fresh root ginger

1 tbsp chopped fresh parsley

1 small red or green chilli, seeded and finely chopped

1 medium red pepper, seeded and diced

1 tsp sea salt

1 tsp freshly ground black pepper

Lemon or lime slices, to garnish

Mixed Nut Balls

Serving suggestion

Serve on individual plates on a bed of chopped lettuce.
Garnish with slices of lemon and hand round your favorite
sauce in a separate bowl.

Variations

Use ground walnuts in place of pecan nuts. Use 1 shallot
in place of the onion. Use 1 yellow or green pepper in
place of the red pepper.

light meals & snacks

29

Method

Remove any grit or stones from the lentils and rinse well. Place in a pan, cover with plenty of water, then bring to the boil and simmer for about 20 minutes, taking care not to overcook. Meanwhile, place the bulgur wheat in a mixing bowl and cover with boiling water. Leave for about 10 minutes – the grain will then have swollen, softened and absorbed the water. Drain off any excess water. Seed and dice the peppers and finely chop the onion.

Drain the cooked lentils and add to the bulgur wheat, together with the peppers, onion, pine nuts, herbs, lemon rind and juice and salt and pepper to taste. Mix well. Using one large lettuce leaf per person, spoon the bulgur wheat salad into the center of the leaves and arrange on a large serving dish garnished with wedges of lemon. Serve.

Bulgur Boats

Ingredients

2 oz green lentils

4 oz bulgur wheat

1 red pepper

1 green pepper

1 onion

2 oz pine nuts (dry roasted in a pan)

2 tsp dried salad herbs (tarragon, chives or parsley)

Rind and juice of 1 lemon

Salt and freshly ground black pepper

4–6 Cos lettuce leaves, to serve

Wedges of lemon, to garnish

Serving suggestion

Serve with fresh crusty bread.

Variations

Use cashew nuts or peanuts in place of pine nuts. Use 1–2 tbsp chopped fresh mixed herbs in place of dried herbs.

Method

Top and tail the okra, then blanch in a saucepan of boiling water for about 3 minutes. Place the okra in a colander, sprinkle with vinegar, then drain well and set aside. Heat the oil in a frying pan, add the okra and onions and cook until the okra change color and the onion softens, stirring continuously.

Add the tomatoes, salt and pepper and parsley to the pan, then add the stock.

Bring to the boil, cover, then reduce the heat and simmer for 10–15 minutes, until the vegetables are cooked and tender, stirring occasionally.

Serve hot, garnished with fresh parsley sprigs.

Ingredients

2 lb 4 oz okra

3 tbsp spiced vinegar

2 tbsp olive oil

2 onions, thinly sliced

10 tomatoes, skinned and chopped

Salt and freshly ground black pepper

3 tbsp chopped fresh parsley

1 3/4 cups vegetable stock

Fresh parsley sprigs, to garnish

Indonesian-Style Okra

Serving suggestions

Serve with warm ciabatta or oven-baked potatoes.

Variations

Use sesame oil in place of olive oil. Use fresh basil in place of parsley.

Method

Break the cauliflower and broccoli into small florets and steam over a saucepan of boiling water for about 7–10 minutes, until just tender. Melt the margarine in a pan, remove from the heat and gradually add the flour. Stir to form a roux, then add the milk gradually, blending well to ensure a smooth consistency. Return the pan to the heat and stir until the sauce thickens and comes to the boil. Remove from the heat. Cool a little, then add the cheese and egg yolk. Stir well and add the nutmeg. In a bowl, whisk the egg white until stiff, then fold carefully into the sauce. Place the steamed vegetables into 6 small buttered ramekin dishes and season with salt and pepper. Divide the sauce evenly between the dishes and bake immediately in a pre-heated oven at 375°F for about 35 minutes, until puffed and golden. Serve at once.

Cauliflower and Broccoli Souflettes

Ingredients

12 oz cauliflower

12 oz broccoli

2 oz vegetable margarine

2 oz brown rice flour

1 3/4 cups milk

2 oz Cheddar cheese, grated

1 large egg, separated

A good pinch of ground nutmeg

Salt and freshly ground black pepper

Serving suggestion

Serve with a mixed green side salad.

Method

Melt the butter in a pan, add the onion and cook until softened, stirring occasionally. Drain the mushrooms, finely chop, then add to the pan. Cook for about 5 minutes, stirring occasionally. Add the Cognac and 1 clove garlic. Increase the heat and cook until the juices in the pan are reduced, stirring frequently.

Stir in the parsley, remove the pan from the heat and set aside to cool.

In a bowl, mix the flour with the milk and cream, then stir in the mushroom mixture, shallots and peppercorns. Mold the mixture together and form into dumplings. Cook the dumplings in a saucepan of salted, boiling water for 10–15 minutes. Drain well and set aside to cool. Meanwhile, wash the spinach and cook in a saucepan with the olive oil without adding any water until wilted.

Drain well and squeeze out any excess water. Chop the cooked spinach.

Add the remaining garlic and season with salt and pepper to taste.

Allow the spinach to cool, then mix with the quark and creme fraiche.

Serve the dumplings with the creamed spinach alongside. Garnish with fresh herb sprigs.

Ingredients

2 tbsp butter

2 onions, thinly sliced

8-oz can mushrooms

1 tbsp Cognac

2 cloves garlic, thinly sliced

6 tbsp chopped fresh parsley

6 oz plain flour

About 1 cup milk

½ cup double cream

2 tbsp finely chopped shallots

1 tbsp green peppercorns

10 ½ oz fresh spinach leaves

1 tbsp olive oil

Salt and freshly ground black pepper

9 oz quark (low-fat curd cheese)

5 ½ oz creme fraiche

Fresh herb sprigs, to garnish

Mushroom Dumplings with Creamed Spinach

Variations

Use broccoli florets in place of spinach leaves and boil for

5 minutes until tender. Mash well before adding the remaining

ingredients. Use canned sweetcorn kernels in place of mush-

rooms. Use chopped fresh basil in place of parsley.

Method

In a bowl, sift together the flour, baking powder, salt and pepper.

Beat the egg in a small bowl and mix with the milk and melted butter.

Stir the egg mixture into the dry ingredients. Stir in the cooked parsnips and mix well. Divide the mixture into 16 equal portions and shape into small fritters. Heat the oil or clarified butter in a frying pan. Fry the fritters in batches until browned on both sides, turning occasionally. Serve hot.

Parsnip Fritters

Ingredients

4 oz plain unbleached flour

2 tsp baking powder

1 tsp salt

½ tsp freshly ground black pepper

1 medium egg

3/4 cup milk

1 tbsp melted butter

1 lb 9 oz cooked parsnips, finely diced

Oil or clarified butter, for frying

Serving suggestions

Serve with yogurt sauce or make them slightly larger and serve as a main course with salad.

Variations

Zucchini, sweetcorn, onions or eggplant can be used in place of the parsnips.

Method

Drain the quark thoroughly. In a bowl, mix the quark with the flour, salt, pepper, nutmeg and prepared vegetables. Mix the wheat grains and pearly barley with the sunflower seeds and add to the quark mixture. Mix well. Heat the margarine in a frying pan, then add the grain mixture. Spread out over the base of the pan and fry for about 5 minutes, until it has formed a crust, then turn and fry the other side until crispy. Break apart with 2 forks and fry the pieces for a further 2 minutes. Sprinkle with the grated cheese to serve.

Ingredients

12 oz quark (low-fat curd cheese)

7 oz plain wholemeal flour

1 tsp salt

Freshly ground black pepper, to taste

Grated nutmeg, to taste

1 bunch of spring onions, finely sliced

1 bulb of fennel, sliced

6 oz wheat grains, cooked

6 oz pearl barley, cooked

1 3/4 oz sunflower seeds

3 tbsp vegetable margarine

3 ½ oz Emmenthal cheese, grated

Mixed Grain Patties

Serving suggestions

Serve with a mixed dark leaf salad or a mixed pepper,
tomato and onion salad.

Variations

Use pumpkin or sesame seeds in place of sunflower
seeds. Use white flour in place of wholemeal flour. Use
Cheddar cheese in place of Emmenthal.

Method

Cook the spaghetti in a large pan of boiling salted water for about 15 minutes, or until al dente. Rinse with cold water, drain well, then lay out flat on a board so that the spaghetti does not stick together. Set aside. Meanwhile, steam the carrots over a pan of boiling water for about 30 minutes, until very tender. Purée the carrots in a food processor or blender until smooth.

In a bowl, mix the carrots with 3 eggs, the creme fraiche and cornflour. Stir the garlic into the mixture with the basil, soy sauce and salt and pepper to taste. Set aside. Meanwhile, heat 1 tbsp oil in a pan and fry the mushrooms with a little salt for about 5 minutes, until the liquid has evaporated, stirring occasionally. Add the mushrooms and tofu to the carrot mixture, stir well, then set aside. Beat the remaining egg, then coat the spaghetti thoroughly in the beaten egg. Line an ovenproof dish with cooking foil and brush with some of the remaining oil. rrange some of the spaghetti on the dish in spirals against the edge of the dish. Spoon in the carrot mixture and press so that the spaghetti is held firmly in place against the sides of the dish. Top with the remaining spaghetti, then cover with cooking foil that has been coated with the remaining oil. Bake in a preheated oven at 425°F for 30–45 minutes, until cooked. When cooked, remove the foil, carefully remove the pasty from the dish and remove the foil from underneath it. Place on a serving plate and keep warm. Meanwhile, for the cheese sauce, pour the milk into a pan and season with salt and pepper and nutmeg. Add the cheese and cook gently, stirring continuously, until the sauce becomes creamy and is hot. Serve the spaghetti pasty with the cheese sauce alongside. Garnish with fresh herb sprigs.

Ingredients

10 ½ oz wholemeal spaghetti

2 lb 4 oz carrots, sliced

4 medium eggs, beaten

3 tbsp creme fraiche

3 tbsp cornflour

1 clove garlic, thinly sliced

2 tbsp chopped fresh basil

1–2 tbsp soy sauce

Salt and freshly ground black pepper

2–3 tbsp sunflower oil

1 lb 2 oz button mushrooms

7 oz tofu, cut into small cubes

Spaghetti Pasty

14 fl oz milk

Ground nutmeg, to taste

4 ½ oz Cheddar cheese

Fresh herbs sprigs, to garnish

Serving suggestion

Serve with cooked fresh vegetables such as green beans and sweetcorn.

main dishes

Method

Wash the lentils thoroughly under cold running water, then drain well. Place the lentils in a bowl, cover with water and leave to soak overnight.

Heat the oil in a pan, add the garlic and cook until softened. Add the prepared vegetables and cook briefly, stirring. Stir in the tomato purée and stock, then bring to the boil. Drain the lentils thoroughly, add to the pan and stir well. Cover and simmer for 30–40 minutes, until the vegetables and lentils are almost cooked and tender, stirring occasionally. Stir in the wine vinegar and thyme. Season with salt and pepper and cayenne, then stir in the honey. Continue cooking over a moderate heat for a further 10–15 minutes, stirring occasionally. Meanwhile, finely chop the chives, leaving a few leaves whole for garnishing. Once the dish is cooked, adjust the seasoning and serve sprinkled with chopped chives. Garnish with slices of leek and whole chive leaves.

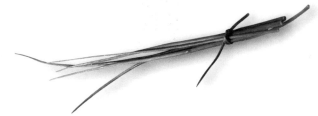

Red Lentils with Vegetables

Ingredients

14 oz red lentils

2 tbsp olive oil

2 cloves garlic, crushed

1 onion, cut into small chunks

1 carrot, cut into small chunks

1 leek, cut into small chunks

1 stick celery, cut into small chunks

2–3 tbsp tomato purée

3 cups vegetable stock

2 tbsp white wine vinegar

1 sprig of fresh thyme

Salt and freshly ground black pepper

A pinch of cayenne pepper

2 tbsp honey

1 bunch of fresh chives

Slices of leek, to garnish

Serving suggestions

Serve with French bread and a green salad or cooked fresh vegetables such as broccoli and carrots.

Method

Cook the lentils in plenty of water in a saucepan until soft. Drain and reserve the liquid and lentils separately. Meanwhile, fry the eggplant in the oil in a pan until lightly browned. Drain well and set aside. Sauté the onion, garlic, carrot, celery and a little of the lentil stock in a pan. Simmer with the lid on until just tender, stirring occasionally. Add the lentils, mixed herbs and canned tomatoes. Simmer gently for 3–4 minutes. Season with shoyu and pepper.

Place a layer of the lentil mixture in a large casserole dish and cover with half the eggplant slices. Cover the eggplant slices with half the potato slices and all the tomato slices. Repeat with the remaining lentils, eggplants and potatoes. For the sauce, melt the margarine in a saucepan, remove from the heat and stir in the flour to form a roux. Add the milk gradually, blending well so that the sauce is smooth. Return to the heat and stir continuously until the sauce thickens. Remove the pan from the heat and cool slightly. Add the egg yolk, stir in the cheese and add the nutmeg. Whisk the egg white in a bowl until stiff, then carefully fold into the sauce. Pour the sauce over the moussaka, covering the dish completely. Bake in a preheated oven at 350°F for about 40 minutes, until the top is golden brown and puffy. Serve hot, garnished with fresh herb sprigs.

Ingredients

5 oz whole green lentils

1 large eggplant, sliced

4–5 tbsp olive oil

1 large onion, chopped

1 clove garlic, crushed

1 large carrot, diced

4 sticks celery, finely chopped

1–2 tsp dried mixed herbs

14–oz can chopped tomatoes

2 tsp shoyu (Japanese soy sauce)

Freshly ground black pepper, to taste

2 medium potatoes, cooked and sliced

2 large tomatoes, sliced

For the sauce

4 tbsp vegetable margarine

2 oz brown rice flour

1 3/4 cups milk

1 large egg, separated

2 oz grated Cheddar cheese

Lentil Moussaka

1 tsp ground nutmeg

Fresh herb sprigs, to garnish

Serving suggestion

Serve with a crunchy green salad.

Variations

Use whole brown lentils in place of green.

Use sweet potatoes in place of standard potatoes.

Method

Heat the oil in a saucepan or paella pan and fry the onion and garlic until soft. Add the paprika and rice and continue to cook for 4–5 minutes, until the rice is transparent, stirring occasionally. Add the stock, wine, tomatoes, tomato purée and herbs and simmer for 10–15 minutes, stirring occasionally.

Add the peppers, celery, mushrooms and mangetout and continue to cook for a further 30 minutes, until the rice is cooked, stirring occasionally. Add a little extra stock, if necessary. Add the peas, cashew nuts and seasoning to taste. Cook until the peas are cooked, then place on a large heated serving dish. Sprinkle the parsley over the top and garnish with lemon wedges and olives. Serve.

Ingredients

4 tbsp olive oil	1 tsp dried oregano
1 large onion, chopped	1 red pepper, seeded and roughly chopped
2 cloves garlic, crushed	1 green pepper, seeded and roughly chopped
½ tsp paprika	3 sticks celery, finely chopped
12 oz long-grain brown rice	8 oz mushrooms, sliced
3 quarts vegetable stock	2 oz mangetout, topped, tailed and cut in half
3/4 cup dry white wine	4 oz frozen peas
14-oz can tomatoes, plus juice, chopped	2 oz cashew nut pieces
1 tbsp tomato purée	Salt and freshly ground black pepper
½ tsp dried tarragon	Chopped fresh parsley, lemon wedges and olives, to garnish
1 tsp dried basil	

Vegetarian Paella

Serving suggestion

Serve with crusty French bread and a mixed dark leaf salad.

Variations

Use a mixture of brown and wild rice for a change. Use unsweet-

ened apple juice in place of white wine. Use fresh wild mushrooms

in place of cultivated mushrooms.

Cook's tip

To prepare in advance, undercook slightly, add

a little more stock or water and reheat.

main dishes

Method

Grind all the spices together using a pestle and mortar. This amount will make 3 tbsp curry powder. Set aside. In a saucepan, fry the onions in the oil until golden, stirring occasionally. Add the ground spices, lower the heat and cook for 3 minutes, stirring continuously. Add the milk and vinegar and stir well.

Add the liquidized tomatoes, tomato purée, sugar and stock. Bring to the boil, cover and simmer gently for 1 hour, stirring occasionally. Add the vegetables and cook for about 30 minutes, until tender, stirring occasionally. Serve.

Serving suggestion Serve with boiled brown rice, chappatis and cucumber raita made by combining diced cucumber with plain yogurt, a little chopped fresh mint, a pinch of chilli powder, ground cumin and seasoning to taste.

Indian Vegetable Curry

Ingredients

2 tsp ground turmeric

1 tsp cumin seeds

1 tsp mustard seeds

1 tsp fenugreek seeds

4 tsp coriander seeds

½ tsp chilli powder

1 tsp ground ginger

1 tsp black peppercorns

1 lb onions, finely chopped

About 4 tbsp vegetable oil

1 ½ cups sterilized milk

2 tbsp white wine vinegar

14-oz can tomatoes, liquidized with their juice

1 tbsp tomato purée

2 tsp brown sugar

1 tsp vegetable bouillon powder or 1 vegetable stock cube dissolved in a little boiling water

2 lb chopped mushrooms or mixed vegetables such as mushrooms, cauliflower, carrots, potatoes and okra

Variations

Use 2–3 tbsp ready-prepared curry powder if preferred.

Method

Cook the lasagne in a large pan of boiling salted water for 8–10 minutes, until al dente. Drain well and drape over a cooling rack or the sides of a colander to cool and prevent sticking together. Meanwhile, in a pan, soften the onion in the oil, sprinkling with a little salt to draw out the juice, then add the garlic. Add the beans, pepper, tomatoes, tomato purée and dried herbs and stir to mix. Simmer for about 10 minutes, or until the vegetables are tender, stirring occasionally. Stir in the shoyu and season to taste. Meanwhile, for the sauce, combine the margarine or butter, flour and milk in a pan. Gradually bring to the boil, whisking continuously. When thickened, allow to simmer, partly covered, for about 6 minutes, stirring frequently. Stir the cheese, if using, into the sauce and season. Layer the lasagne in a greased dish in the following order: half the bean mix, half the pasta, the remainder of the bean mix, then the remainder of the pasta. Top with the sauce. Bake in a preheated oven at 350°F for about 35 minutes, or until golden brown and bubbling.

Serve in the dish in which it has been cooked and garnish with fresh herb sprigs.

Ingredients

8 sheets wholemeal lasagne

1 large onion, finely chopped

1 tbsp vegetable oil

Salt

1–2 cloves garlic, crushed

8 oz cooked aduki beans

1 green pepper, seeded and chopped

14-oz can chopped tomatoes

1 tbsp tomato purée

1 tsp dried basil

1 tsp dried oregano

Shoyu (Japanese soy sauce) or salt

Freshly ground black pepper

For the sauce

2 tbsp vegetable margarine or butter

1 oz plain wholemeal flour

1 3/4 cups cold dairy or soya milk

2 oz Cheddar cheese, grated (optional)

Fresh herbs sprigs, to garnish

Beany Lasagne

Serving suggestion

Serve with a green salad and crusty fresh bread.

Variations

Use lasagne verde in place of wholemeal lasagne. Use
other cooked beans such as black-eye or flageolet in
place of aduki beans.

Method

In a pan, fry the onion and garlic in the oil until soft, stirring occasionally. Remove from the heat. In a bowl, mix together the onion and garlic with all the remaining ingredients, except the garnish, and season to taste with salt and pepper. Mix well. Place the mixture in a greased 2-lb loaf tin and level the surface. Cover with foil and bake in a preheated oven at 350°F for 1 hour. Remove the foil and bake for a further 10 minutes.

Leave to stand in the baking tin for at least 10 minutes before turning out.

Turn out onto a serving plate and serve in slices, garnished with fresh parsley sprigs and pepper slices.

Carrot and Cashew Nut Roast

Ingredients

1 medium onion, chopped

1–2 cloves garlic, crushed

1 tbsp olive or sunflower oil

1 lb carrots, cooked and mashed

8 oz cashew nuts, ground

4 oz fresh wholemeal breadcrumbs

1 tbsp light tahini

1 ½ tsp caraway seeds

1 tsp yeast extract

Juice of ½ lemon

1/3 cup stock from the carrots or water

Salt and freshly ground black pepper

Fresh parsley sprigs and pepper slices, to garnish

Serving suggestions

Serve hot with roast potatoes and a green vegetable such as cabbage, or cold with a mixed green salad and garlic or herb-flavored bread.

Method

Lay the potato and zucchini slices overlapping in a greased soufflé dish.

In a bowl, mix the crushed garlic with the cream. Season to taste with salt and pepper. Stir in the chopped tarragon, then pour the mixture evenly over the vegetables. Sprinkle over the grated cheese and dot with the butter.

Bake in a preheated oven at 425°F for 20–25 minutes, until cooked and golden brown. Serve hot.

Ingredients

9 oz cooked potatoes, sliced

9 oz zucchini, sliced

2 cloves garlic, crushed

1 cup double cream

Freshly ground sea salt and black pepper

1–2 tbsp chopped fresh tarragon

1 3/4 oz grated Emmenthal cheese

A knob of butter

Potato and Zucchini Gratin

Serving suggestion

Serve with a crisp green salad and crusty

French bread or ciabatta.

Variations

Use sweet potatoes in place of standard potatoes. Use mush-

rooms in place of zucchinis. Use Cheddar cheese in place of

Emmenthal. Use fresh basil or parsley in place of tarragon.

main dishes

Method

Mix the bulgur wheat with the salt in a bowl, pour over 1 ½ cups water and leave for 15–20 minutes. All the water will then be absorbed. Meanwhile, whisk together all the ingredients for the dressing in a small bowl, then pour over the soaked bulgur. Fold in lightly with a spoon. Cover and leave for 2 hours, or overnight in the refrigerator or a cool place. Add the tomatoes, cucumber and spring onions to the bulgur wheat and mix well. Serve, garnished with fresh mint sprigs.

Tabouleh

Ingredients

6–7 oz bulgur wheat

1 tsp salt

1 lb tomatoes, chopped

½ cucumber, diced

3–4 spring onions, chopped

Fresh mint sprigs, to garnish

For the dressing

¼ cup olive oil

¼ cup fresh lemon juice

2 tbsp chopped fresh mint

4 tbsp chopped fresh parsley

2 cloves garlic, crushed

Variations

Use cooked couscous or rice in place of bulgur wheat. Use plum tomatoes in place of standard potatoes. Use walnut or hazelnut oil in place of olive oil. Use fresh lime or orange juice in place of lemon juice.

Cook's tip

A few cooked beans can be added to make this dish more substantial.

Method

Scrub the potatoes with a brush. Remove and discard the roots and darker green foliage from the spring onions and cut in half lengthways. Heat the oil in a pan, add the potatoes and cook until evenly lightly browned all over, stirring frequently. Add the spring onions and garlic and cook for about 5 minutes, stirring occasionally. Season with salt and pepper and sprinkle with the thyme.

Add a little water and cook for a further 10–15 minutes, until the potatoes are cooked and tender, stirring occasionally. Serve hot.

Ingredients

1 lb 2 oz baby new potatoes

1 bunch of spring onions

2 tbsp olive oil

10 small fresh cloves garlic

Salt and freshly ground black pepper

1 tbsp finely chopped fresh thyme

Garlic Baby New Potatoes

Serving suggestion

Serve as an accompaniment to grilled or roast mixed vegetables, such as eggplant, peppers and zucchini.

Variations

Use sesame oil in place of olive oil. Use fresh marjoram, oregano or chives in place of thyme.

Cook's tip

Do not let the garlic brown too much, or it will taste bitter.

vegetables & salads

Method

Remove and discard the skin from the cucumbers, then cut in half lengthways. Remove and discard the seeds with a spoon and cut the flesh into slices about ½-inch thick. Melt the butter in a pan, add the spring onions and cook for 5 minutes, until softened, stirring occasionally..Add the cucumber and cook gently for 3 minutes, stirring occasionally. Add the pepper to the cucumber mixture and cook for 5 minutes, until softened, stirring occasionally.

Add the lemon rind and juice and salt and pepper to taste. Cover the pan and cook gently for a further 7 minutes, stirring occasionally.

Stir in the cream, then cook briefly over a higher heat before adding the wine.

Sprinkle with chopped dill before serving. Serve hot.

Cucumber in a Creamy Dill Sauce

Ingredients

2–3 cucumbers, weighing about 1 lb 12 oz in total

1 tbsp butter

1 bunch of spring onions, trimmed and sliced

1 red pepper, seeded and cut into small pieces

Finely grated rind and juice of 1 lemon

Salt and white pepper

8 tbsp double cream

2 tbsp dry white wine

1–2 tbsp chopped fresh dill

Serving suggestions

Serve with cheese-topped oven-baked potatoes and fresh crusty bread or grilled polenta.

Variations

Use fresh mint in place of dill. Use lime rind and juice in place of lemon. Use crème fraîche in place of cream.

Method

Core, seed and thinly slice the peppers. Slice the tomatoes and onions.

Arrange the peppers, tomatoes and onions alternately on a round serving dish and sprinkle the lentil sprouts over the top. In a bowl, whisk all the ingredients for the dressing together thoroughly and pour over the vegetables.

Cover and leave to marinate for at least 1 hour at room temperature before serving.

Just before serving, garnish with halved black grapes and serve.

Green Pepper Salad

Ingredients

3 medium green peppers

3 medium tomatoes

2 medium onions

3 oz sprouted lentils

Black grapes, to garnish

For the dressing

4 tbsp olive oil

2 tbsp red wine vinegar

2 tsp ground cumin

½ tsp chopped fresh coriander

Cook's tips

Make sure you only sprout whole lentils – red split lentils will not sprout. You can prepare this salad in advance and refrigerate until required, but remove from the refrigerator 30 minutes before serving.

Method

Cut the carrots into matchstick strips. Set aside. Seed and thinly slice the pepper. Set aside. Cut the apricots into slivers. Set aside. Toast the sesame seeds in a dry pan over a low heat until golden brown. Remove from the heat and set aside. Place the carrots, pepper, apricots and beansprouts in a serving dish. Mix the French dressing with the pineapple juice in a bowl and fold into the salad. Sprinkle the sesame seeds over the top and serve at once.

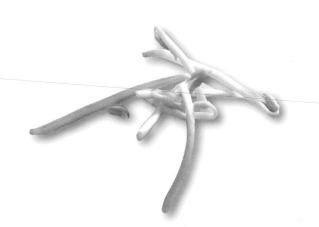

Mount Carmel Salad

Serving suggestions

Serve as an accompaniment to vegetable flans or pizzas, or with fresh crusty bread.

Ingredients

4 oz carrots, peeled

1 green pepper

2 oz fresh apricots

1 tbsp sesame seeds

8 oz beansprouts

4 tbsp French dressing

2 tbsp unsweetened pineapple juice

Variations

Use pumpkin or sunflower seeds in place of sesame seeds.

Use apple or orange juice in place of pineapple juice.

Cook's tip

Use beansprouts which are at least 1 inch long for this recipe.

Method

Seed the pepper and cut into matchstick pieces. Set aside. Trim the broccoli and cauliflower and break into small florets. Place the pepper, broccoli and cauliflower in a mixing bowl. For the dressing, combine the yogurt, lemon juice, oil, salt and pepper and nutmeg in a clean screw-top jar and shake well.

Pour the dressing over the salad and toss together to mix well. Divide the mixture between 4 individual serving plates or bowls and garnish with the almond flakes. Serve.

Ingredients

1 red pepper

10 oz broccoli

10 oz cauliflower

1 tbsp toasted flaked almonds

For the dressing

4 tbsp Greek yogurt

2 tbsp fresh lemon juice

2 tbsp olive oil

Broccoli and Cauliflower Salad

Salt and freshly ground black pepper

A pinch of ground nutmeg

Serving suggestions

Serve with crackers, oatcakes or crusty fresh bread.

Variations

Omit the nutmeg from the dressing and add a few chopped fresh herbs. Use cherry tomatoes or button mushrooms in place of cauliflower. Use fresh lime juice in place of lemon juice.

vegetables & salads

Method

Heat the olive oil in a pan and cook the zucchini until lightly browned all over, stirring occasionally. Sprinkle with dill. Pour the cooking liquid into a bowl and add the walnut oil, lemon juice, vinegar, pepper and salt and sugar.

Mix well and set aside. Slice the tomatoes, slice the peppers into strips, then slice the onions into rings. Add the tomatoes, peppers and onions to the marinade and mix well. Add the zucchini slices, feta and herbs to the marinade and mix all the ingredients together thoroughly. Cover and leave to marinate in the refrigerator for about 1 hour. Before serving, shred the lettuce leaves, then mix with the salad. Serve immediately.

Greek Salad

Ingredients

4 tbsp olive oil

4 small zucchinis, sliced

1 tbsp finely chopped fresh dill

2 tbsp walnut oil

2 tbsp fresh lemon juice

1 tbsp tarragon vinegar

Salt and freshly ground black pepper, to taste

Sugar, to taste

4 large tomatoes, skinned

1 red pepper, seeded

1 green pepper, seeded

2 onions

9 oz feta cheese, crumbled

2 tbsp finely chopped fresh parsley

1 tsp finely chopped fresh mint or lemon balm

1 head of lettuce

Variations

Use red onions in place of standard onions. Use hazelnut or olive oil in place of walnut oil. Use other herb-flavored vinegars in place of tarragon vinegar. Use Cheddar or Mozzarella cheese in place of feta cheese.

Method

Sift the flour into a bowl. Add the milk, stir in the sugar, then crumble the yeast into the mixture. Mix to a smooth dough, knead gently, then leave to rise for 10–15 minutes. Add the butter, 2 whole eggs, salt and 1–2 tbsp) of the oil to the dough and work into the dough until well mixed and smooth. Cover the dough and set aside in a warm place for about 30 minutes to rise. Knead the dough once more and set aside for a further 30 minutes. Divide the dough into about 12 small balls, then roll each out on a lightly floured work surface.

Grease a baking sheet with the remaining oil. Place the dough balls on the baking sheet and flatten each one out slightly. In a bowl, beat the egg yolks with 4 tbsp water and brush the dough balls with the mixture. Sprinkle the dough balls with caraway seeds, salt and coriander seeds. Leave for a further 10 minutes to rise. Bake in a preheated oven at 350°F for 15–20 minutes, until risen, cooked and golden brown. Serve warm or cold.

Ingredients

1 lb 2 oz strong white flour

½ cup lukewarm milk

A large pinch of sugar

1 oz fresh yeast

½ cup butter, at room temperature

2 medium eggs, plus 2 egg yolks

1 tbsp salt

2–3 tbsp olive oil

1 tbsp caraway seeds

1 tbsp coarse sea salt

1 tbsp coriander seeds

Mixed Seed Bread Rolls

Serving suggestions

Serve with butter, savory spread or vegetarian paté.

Variations

Use wholemeal flour or a mixture of white and wholemeal flour in place of all

white flour. Use cumin, poppy or sesame seeds in place of caraway seeds.

Method

Wash the potatoes, then cook in a large saucepan of lightly salted, boiling water for about 20 minutes, until tender. Peel the potatoes while they are still hot, then mash well. Set aside. Dissolve the yeast in 2–3 tbsp lukewarm water in a bowl. Mix the yeast with the flour in a large bowl, then add the milk, a further cup lukewarm water and the butter. Add the salt, then knead well to form a smooth dough. Peel and core the apple, then finely grate.

Heat all but 2 tbsp of the sunflower seeds in a pan without any oil or fat for 5 minutes, then knead into the dough, together with the mashed potatoes and grated apple. Place the dough in a bowl, cover and set aside in a warm place for about 1 ½ hours to rise. Grease two 1 lb loaf tins, divide the dough equally between them, then sprinkle with the remaining 2 tbsp sunflower seeds and leave to rise in a warm place for a further 40 minutes. Bake in a preheated oven at 425°F for about 40–50 minutes, until cooked. When cooked, turn the bread out of the tins on its side and place on a wire rack to cool. Serve in slices.

Autumn Loaf

Ingredients

1 lb 2 oz floury potatoes

1 ½ oz fresh yeast, crumbled

1 lb 2 oz plain strong wholemeal flour

1 cup lukewarm milk

3 tbsp butter, softened

1 tsp sea salt

1 apple

5 ½ oz sunflower seeds

Serving suggestions

Serve in slices, warm or cold, spread with a little butter, vegetable margarine or savory vegetable paté.

Variations

Use sweet potatoes in place of standard potatoes. Use pumpkin, sesame or poppy seeds in place of sunflower seeds. Use 1 pear in place of the apple.

Method

Grate the carrots into a bowl and sprinkle with lemon juice. Set aside.In a separate bowl, mix the flour thoroughly with the yeast, then add the flaked grains, ground almonds, salt, honey, butter, egg and ½ cup lukewarm water and work in the ingredients to form a smooth dough. Knead the dough for about 5 minutes. While kneading, add the grated carrot a little at a time.

Add the raisins and knead well. Place the dough in a bowl, cover and leave in a warm place until risen to about double its original volume. Knead once more on a lightly floured work surface. Sprinkle half the blanched almonds over the base of a greased soufflé dish and place the dough on top. Sprinkle the remaining almonds over the top of the dough. Press the dough gently down into the dish, then cover and leave in a warm place once again until risen to double its volume. Bake in a preheated oven at 400°F for 50–55 minutes, until cooked.

Turn out onto a wire rack to cool and serve in slices.

Almond and Carrot Bread

Ingredients

10 ½ oz carrots

1–2 tbsp lemon juice

1 lb 2 oz strong white flour

1 sachet dried yeast

3 tbsp flaked wholewheat grains

3 ½ oz ground almonds

1 tsp sea salt

3 tbsp honey

½ cup butter, softened

1 medium egg, beaten

5 ½ oz golden raisins

1 ½ oz blanched almonds

Variations

Use zucchini in place of carrots. Use ground and blanched hazelnuts in place of almonds. Use chopped ready-to-eat dried apricots in place of raisins.

Method

Cook the oatmeal in a pan without oil or fat until golden, stirring frequently. Remove from the heat and set aside to cool. Finely chop the prunes, sultanas and hazelnuts. Heat the butter and syrup in a pan until melted, remove from the heat and set aside to cool. Add salt and the lemon rind to the mineral water in a jug and mix with the yeast. Place the flour in a bowl, add the chopped fruit and nuts, the butter and syrup mixture and the oatmeal and yeast mixture. Knead together thoroughly to form a smooth dough. Cover and leave the dough overnight in the refrigerator. Using 2 spoons, place small balls of the dough on baking sheets lined with greaseproof or non-stick baking paper. Bake in a preheated oven at 400°F for 20–25 minutes, until golden brown and cooked. Transfer to a wire rack to cool. Mix the honey with 2 tbsp boiling water in a bowl and brush the cooled cookies with the honey mixture. Leave to dry, then serve.

Muesli Cookies

Ingredients

4 ½ oz coarse oatmeal

3 ½ oz stoned prunes

3 ½ oz golden raisins

3 ½ oz hazelnuts

½ cup butter

1 cup golden syrup

A pinch of sea salt

Finely grated rind of 1 lemon

½ cup mineral water

4 ½ oz crumbled fresh yeast

4 ½ oz strong white flour

2 tbsp honey

Serving suggestion

Serve as a treat or snack with a glass of sparkling apple juice.

Variations

Use ready-to-eat dried pears or peaches or figs in place of prunes. Use almonds or walnuts in place of hazelnuts. Use lime rind in place of lemon rind.

Cook's tip

A quick and easy way to chop dried fruit such as prunes is to snip them into pieces using a clean pair of kitchen scissors.

Method

Sift the flour and baking powder into a bowl and mix well. Make a well in the center and add the 5 ½ oz sugar, vanilla sugar, salt and egg and mix well.

Rub in the butter a little at a time and gradually knead the mixture to form a smooth dough. Set aside about one third of the dough. Add the cocoa powder, the remaining 1 tbsp powdered sugar, milk or rum and the chopped almonds to the remaining dough, kneading well. Form the dough into 4 rectangular sausage shapes about 12 ½ inches long, 1 ¼ inches wide and about 5/8 inch thick.

Roll out the reserved dough to about 17 ½ inches by 12 ½ inches and cut into 4 strips, each about 4 ¼ inches by 12 ½ inches. Brush the dough with a little egg white and place one sausage of almond-flavored dough on each piece of plain dough and wrap the plain dough around the flavored dough, enclosing it completely. Wrap each loaf in aluminium foil and chill overnight in the refrigerator. Unwrap the loaves, cut into ½-inch slices and place on greased baking trays covered with greaseproof or non-stick baking paper. Bake in a preheated oven at 400°F for 12–15 minutes, until cooked. Transfer to a wire rack to cool before serving.

Chocolate and Almond Biscuits

Ingredients

1 lb 2 oz plain white flour

2 tsp baking powder

5 ½ oz powdered sugar, plus 1 tbsp

½ oz vanilla sugar

A pinch of salt

1 large egg, beaten

12 oz cold butter, diced

1 ½ oz cocoa powder, sifted

1 tbsp milk or rum

3 ½ oz coarsely chopped blanched almonds

A little egg white, for brushing

Serving suggestions

Serve with a glass of dessert wine or freshly squeezed fruit juice.

Variations

Use half white and half wholemeal flour in place of all white flour. Use hazelnuts or pecan nuts in place of almonds.

Method

Break the carob into a pan and add the margarine and honey. Melt over a very low heat and stir until all the ingredients have melted and blended.Remove from the heat and stir in the oats, sultanas and coconut. Spread the mixture evenly into a greased shallow, rectangular 11 x 7 inch baking tin and bake in a preheated oven at 350°F for 25–30 minutes. Cool slightly, then mark into slices. Place on a wire rack to cool. When completely cold, remove from the tin and store in an airtight container.

Choc-Oat Slices

Ingredients

4 oz carob bar

4 oz hard vegetable margarine

1 tbsp clear honey

8 oz porridge oats

4 oz golden raisins

2 oz desiccated coconut

Serving suggestion

Serve with a glass of freshly squeezed orange juice.

Cook's tip

Wrapped in foil or sealed in a container, these slices freeze well for up to 3 months.

Method

Beat the butter in a bowl until creamy, then gradually beat in the sugar, vanilla sugar, eggs, salt and almond essence. Stir in the nuts, then fold in the flour, cornflour and baking powder. Stir in the milk and mix well.

Grease a pudding basin and dust with a little flour. Spoon the almond mixture into the bowl and level the surface. Cover with greaseproof paper and secure with string. Steam in a steamer over a pan of boiling water for 1–1½ hours, or until risen and cooked. Turn out onto a warmed serving plate and serve immediately.

Almond Steamed Pudding

Ingredients

½ cup butter, softened

3 1//2 oz powdered sugar

½ oz vanilla sugar

3 medium eggs

A pinch of salt

2 drops of almond essence

1 3/4 oz almonds or hazelnuts, chopped

5 ½ oz plain flour, sifted

1 3/4 oz cornflour

2 tsp baking powder, sifted

3 tbsp milk

A little flour, for dusting

Serving suggestions

Serve with chocolate sauce or zabaglione.

Variations

Use vanilla essence in place of almond essence. Use currants or raisins in place of nuts. Use half white and half wholemeal flour in place of all white flour.

Method

Finely pare the zest from 3 of the oranges and boil the zest in a little water in a pan for 2 minutes. Remove from the heat, drain and cool. Peel the oranges using a sharp knife, making sure that all the pith is removed. Thinly slice the oranges, arrange in a serving dish and sprinkle the zest over the top. Sprinkle the brandy over the oranges, cover and refrigerate for about 1 hour. Place the mangoes and peaches in a food processor or blender and blend until smooth. Place in a bowl. Stir in the cream, cover and refrigerate until required.

Serve the oranges with the peach and mango cream alongside.

Ingredients

6 large jaffa oranges

3 tbsp brandy

2 mangoes, peeled, stoned and cut into chunks

4 small ripe peaches, peeled, stoned and roughly chopped

3 tbsp double cream

Brandied Oranges
with Peach and Mango Cream

Serving suggestion

Serve with wafer or sponge finger biscuits.

Variations

Use Greek yogurt or crème fraîche in place of double

cream. Use nectarines in place of peaches. Use pink or

ruby grapefruit in place of oranges.

desserts

Method

Cream the margarine and sugar together in a bowl until pale and fluffy.

Beat in the eggs one at a time, then carefully fold in the flour, carob powder and baking powder. Turn into 2 greased 7-inch sponge or flan tins and level the surfaces. Bake in a preheated oven at 350°F for about 20 minutes, until golden brown and risen. Turn out onto a wire rack to cool. Set aside. Place one of the carob sponges in a trifle bowl and pour the apple juice over the sponge. Set aside for 30 minutes. Drizzle over the liqueur, if using, then arrange the prepared fruits and nuts over the sponge, covering it completely. In a bowl, whip the cream until stiff, then fold in the yogurt. Spread evenly over the fruit, covering it completely. With the back of a fork, trace from the rim of the bowl into the center, making a lined effect. Chill before serving. Decorate with orange segments, pineapple cubes and carob chips and serve.

Ingredients

For the carob sponge

4 oz soft vegetable margarine

3 oz light muscovado sugar, finely ground

2 medium eggs

3 oz plain wholemeal flour, sifted

1 oz carob powder

1 ½ tsp baking powder

For the trifle

6 tbsp apple juice

1–2 tbsp apricot or banana liqueur (optional)

2 crisp apples, cored and chopped but not peeled

1 large banana, sliced

2 oranges, segmented and roughly chopped

Half a pineapple, cored and diced

Fruit Salad Trifle

A few grapes, halved and seeded

2 oz fresh dates, stoned and chopped

2 oz hazelnuts, chopped

4 oz whipping cream

4 oz Greek yogurt

Orange segments, pineapple cubes and carob chips, to decorate

Cook's tip

Since this recipes makes two halves of sponge and only one is needed for the trifle, the other half can be frozen or used on a subsequent occasion.

Method

Place all the ingredients, apart from the pineapple, in a food processor or blender and blend until smooth and well mixed. Add the pineapple and blend briefly to mix. Place the mixture in a shallow freezerproof container, cover and freeze for about 2 hours, or until mushy in consistency. Spoon into a chilled bowl and mash with a fork to break down the ice crystals. Return the mixture to the container, cover and freeze until firm. Transfer to the refrigerator for about 30 minutes before serving, to allow the ice cream to soften a little. Serve in scoops.

Ingredients

1 large very ripe banana, roughly chopped

4 oz finely ground cashew nuts

3/4 cup concentrated soya milk

½ tsp vanilla essence

2 tsp clear honey

2 rings unsweetened canned pineapple, diced

Cashew Ice Cream

Serving suggestions

Serve with strawberries or fresh fruit salad.

Variations

Use hazelnuts, almonds or pistachio nuts in place of cashew nuts. Use maple syrup in place of honey. Use almond essence in place of vanilla essence.

desserts

Method

Pit the prunes and roughly chop. Halve the apricots and quarter the figs.

Place all the fruit in a large bowl and add the remaining ingredients. Stir well to mix.

Cover with cold water and stir well. Cover and keep in a cool place for 1–2 days, stirring a couple of times each day. Before serving, mix again thoroughly and spoon into bowls to serve.

Compote

Ingredients

8 oz dried prunes

8 oz dried apricots

4 oz dried figs

4 oz raisins

4 oz blanched almonds

2 oz pine nuts

1 tsp ground cinnamon

¼ tsp ground nutmeg

4 oz light soft brown sugar

1 tbsp rosewater

Finely grated rind and juice of 1 orange

Cook's tip

After 24 hours the liquid in which the compote is soaking will become very thick and syrupy. If you need to add more liquid, add a little orange juice.

Method

Sift the flours into a mixing bowl and add the salt, honey, soured cream and butter. Knead the ingredients together to form a smooth dough. If the dough is sticky, place on a plate in the refrigerator for a while to rest. On a lightly floured work surface, roll out the pastry to a round slightly larger than a 10-inch fluted flan tin and use to line the tin. Trim the edges. Prick a few holes in the pastry base with a fork and place on a baking tray. Bake in a preheated oven at 375°F for 20–25 minutes, until pale golden and cooked. Transfer to a wire rack to cool. Remove the flan case carefully from the tin. Place the cooled flan case on a serving plate. Arrange the fruit in the flan case.

Heat the jam in a saucepan, stirring continuously, until runny, then brush the fruit all over with the jam. Serve in slices, decorated with the chopped nuts.

Ingredients

For the pastry

3½ oz plain white flour

3½ oz buckwheat flour

A pinch of salt

1 tbsp honey

½ cup sour cream

½ cup butter, softened

For the filling

1 lb 5 oz-1 lb 9 oz prepared soft fruit, such as strawberries, raspberries, blackberries or cooked apricots

4 tbsp strawberry or apricot jam

Chopped nuts, to decorate

Mixed Fruit Tart

Serving suggestion

Serve with maple syrup and whipped cream.

Variations

Use your own choice of fruit for this tart, such as mixed tropical fruit or autumn

berries. Use plain wholemeal flour in place of buckwheat flour.

Cook's tip

Individual tartlets may be made instead of 1 large tart. Reduce the cooking time

a little for tartlets.

desserts

Index